Goodbye, Brecken

Published by
MAGINATION PRESS
An Educational Publishing Foundation Book
American Psychological Association
750 First Street, NE
Washington, DC 20002

For more information about our books, including a complete catalog, please write to us,
call 1-800-374-2721, or visit our website at www.apa.org/pubs/magination.

Printed by Worzalla, Stevens Point, WI

Library of Congress Cataloging-in-Publication Data
Lupton, David.
 Goodbye, Brecken : a story about the death of a pet / written and illustrated by David Lupton.
     p. cm.
  ISBN 978-1-4338-1289-7 (hbk. : alk. paper) — ISBN 978-1-4338-1290-3 (pbk. : alk. paper)
1. Loss (Psychology) in children—Juvenile literature. 2. Loss (Psychology)—Juvenile literature.
I. Title.
  BF724.3.L66L87 2013
  155.9'37—dc23
                            2012035892

Manufactured in the United States of America
10 9 8 7 6 5 4 3 2 1

ECO-FRIENDLY BOOKS
Made in the USA

Goodbye, Brecken

A Story About the Death of a Pet

written and illustrated
by David Lupton

Magination Press • Washington, DC
American Psychological Association

This English edition is published by arrangement with EenBook Co., through the ChoiceMaker Korea Co.

Brecken is Isabelle's dog.
Isabelle and Brecken were always together.

They played together and snuggled together.
The two of them were even born on the same day!

When Brecken died, Isabelle's parents told her, "Although you and Brecken are the same age, in animal years he is much older. Brecken must have been too old for his body to live any longer."

Their words gave Isabelle no comfort.

Isabelle was so sad. She cried.
She got angry.
She was so lonely. She missed Brecken so much!

That night when she fell asleep, Isabelle dreamed
she set off on a long journey to find Brecken.

First Isabelle met a deer with big horns.
"Hello. Have you seen my dog, Brecken?"

But the deer did not say anything.
The deer's warm and wet nose felt just like Brecken's.

Isabelle then met a fox with soft red fur.
"Hello. I'm looking for my dog, Brecken."

But the fox just stared at her and did not say anything.
She buried her face in the fox's fur and missed
Brecken even more.

Then some rabbits came up to Isabelle.
"Hello. I'm looking for my dog, Brecken."

They hopped around her.
She remembered the happy times
when she used to play with Brecken.

At that moment, a big black crow flew toward her.
"Hello. I'm looking for my dog, Brecken."

It opened its dark-as-night wings and cawed loudly:
Caw! Caw! Caw!

Then everything disappeared.
Isabelle was alone again.

Isabelle was afraid.

Isabelle lay down on the ground.
Crunch, crunch, crunch…

She felt something licking her face.
"Brecken! It's you!"

Isabelle climbed on Brecken's back and off they ran.

Isabelle could feel Brecken's heart pumping
and his warm body.
Isabelle wasn't afraid anymore.

When Isabelle awoke from her dream, she knew.
Brecken had died. She must say goodbye.

Isabelle will always love Brecken, as he loved her.
Isabelle knew that Brecken lived a long and happy life
and her memories of him will never go away.
Brecken will always be close in her heart.

Isabelle is crying because she misses Brecken.
Color her teardrops.

Isabelle is asking the other animals about Brecken.
Imagine you are Isabelle. Describe Brecken.

Deer, did you see Brecken?
Brecken is _____
_____

Fox, did you see Brecken?
Brecken is _____
_____

Isabelle saw Brecken in a dream again.
Make the dream background magical.

Note to Parents

by Allan Peterkin, MD

For most people, especially children, pets are an integral part of the family. Children often form special bonds with animals, who grow up and play alongside them. For many children, the death of a pet may be the first experience of loss, grief, and the process of mourning. By explaining the loss gently and honestly, and by offering support and practical coping techniques, you can help your child work through his grief.

Explaining a Pet's Death

How you talk to your child about what has happened will depend on her age and developmental level. Toddlers (ages 2-3) may sense tension and change in the family but have no understanding of the permanence of death. Children ages 4-6 may imagine that the pet is still alive somewhere else or use magical thinking with the hope that the pet will return. For example, your child may ask if she can play with the pet tomorrow. You can gently remind her that death is permanent by saying something like, "I'm sorry, but he won't be able to play tomorrow either." Kids 7-9 understand the permanence of death and may have specific, even graphic questions about what happens to the pet's body after death. It's important to answer these questions honestly and tactfully. Adolescents may conceal their feelings, but still be deeply moved by the loss. Don't be fooled by a "cool" or "tough" exterior. Encourage your older children to help their younger siblings navigate the change.

The cause of death is important too. In the case of age and worsening illness, parents can prepare gradually for the loss by explaining how animals age much more quickly than humans and their bodily functions stop working. Visible changes in appearance or behavior can be pointed out over time. Accidents are traumatic for the whole family. The experience is intense and usually shared and talked about.

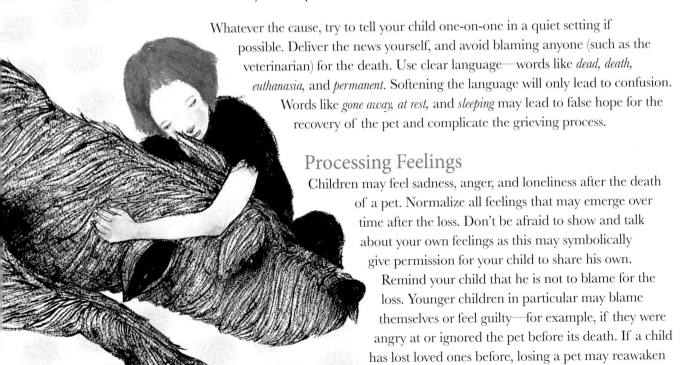

Whatever the cause, try to tell your child one-on-one in a quiet setting if possible. Deliver the news yourself, and avoid blaming anyone (such as the veterinarian) for the death. Use clear language—words like *dead*, *death*, *euthanasia*, and *permanent*. Softening the language will only lead to confusion. Words like *gone away*, *at rest*, and *sleeping* may lead to false hope for the recovery of the pet and complicate the grieving process.

Processing Feelings

Children may feel sadness, anger, and loneliness after the death of a pet. Normalize all feelings that may emerge over time after the loss. Don't be afraid to show and talk about your own feelings as this may symbolically give permission for your child to share his own.

Remind your child that he is not to blame for the loss. Younger children in particular may blame themselves or feel guilty—for example, if they were angry at or ignored the pet before its death. If a child has lost loved ones before, losing a pet may reawaken old feelings and trigger anxieties about someone else in the family becoming ill, dying, or leaving. Be ready to gently make the connection and to help make a distinction between then and now. Respect your child's privacy about his emotions, but let him know you are open to hearing about feelings whenever they emerge. As time goes on, talk about the pet by name and remind family members that it's okay to be sad even a long while after the loss. Other times, fun, happy memories may emerge and it's important to make room for them too. Children, like Isabelle in this story, may have dreams about trying to find the pet. Listen to them and reinforce that dreams can be an important part of working through change and loss for all of us.

Coping Strategies

Gather additional support. Maximize support for your child by informing other adults in the child's life, such as teachers, coaches, and grandparents. People who have never had pets may be dismissive, making remarks like "It's only an animal." Tell them how important the animal was to your child so the loss is not minimized.

Build in ritual to honor the loss. Discuss holding a memorial service and involve your child in planning the details. Will you bury the pet's body? Will you ask for the ashes after cremation at the vet's and bury those? If the body is lost, severely damaged, or left at the veterinary clinic, consider burying some object, like a collar, associated with the pet. Hold a short ceremony and say a few words. Talk about favorite memories. Avoid platitudes. This may be an opportunity for you to talk about your own spiritual views and what you think happens after death. Your child can then let you know what they think happens or whether it makes them anxious to even think about it.

Encourage creative expression. Consider asking your child to draw a picture of the pet, write a goodbye letter to him, create a family scrapbook, or make a clay marker for the grave. Ask if they would like to keep a favorite toy or photo as a memento.

Discuss your next steps together as a family. Don't rush into getting a new pet. Nothing can replace the old one. Planning together, when the time is right, is a way to move forward through the loss while honoring and remembering the pet who has died. You may even decide together to find a different breed or type of animal as your next pet or to adopt a homeless older pet. Discuss all of these options openly and seek family consensus. Make a special occasion of going to select and bring home the new animal.

Hopefully, given time, your child's feelings of loss and grief will transition to acceptance and happy memories. However, if your child's grief persists, becomes overwhelming, or interferes with daily activities, it may be time to seek help from a licensed psychologist or psychotherapist.

Allan Peterkin, MD, is a Toronto-based physician and writer. He is Associate Professor of Psychiatry and Family Medicine and head of Health, Arts, and Humanities at the University of Toronto. Dr. Peterkin is the author of several children's books, including *The Flyaway Blanket* and *What About Me? When Brothers and Sisters Get Sick*, both published by Magination Press.

About the Author and Illustrator

David Lupton was born in South England, and studied illustration in Portsmouth. He currently resides in Edinburgh. He has illustrated for many magazines and for picture books such as *Dreams of Lah* and *Peter and the Wolf.* *Goodbye, Brecken* is the first story he has both written and illustrated.

About Magination Press

Magination Press is an imprint of the American Psychological Association, the largest scientific and professional organization representing psychologists in the United States and the largest association of psychologists worldwide.